POETRY
ESCAPE

POETS FROM THE WEST
MIDLANDS

Edited By Sarah Olivo

First published in Great Britain in 2019 by:

YoungWriters® Est. 1991

Young Writers
Remus House
Coltsfoot Drive
Peterborough
PE2 9BF
Telephone: 01733 890066
Website: www.youngwriters.co.uk

SB ISBN 978-1-78988-167-7
Printed and bound in the UK by BookPrintingUK
Website: www.bookprintinguk.com
YB0392CZ

FOREWORD

Since 1991 our aim here at Young Writers has been to encourage creativity in children and young adults and to inspire a love of the written word. Each competition is tailored to the relevant age group, hopefully giving each student the inspiration and incentive to create their own piece of creative writing, whether it's a poem or a short story. We truly believe that seeing their work in print gives students a sense of achievement and pride.

For our latest competition Poetry Escape, we challenged secondary school students to free their creativity and escape the maze of their minds using poetic techniques as their tools of navigation. They had several pathways to choose from, with each one offering either a specific theme or a writing constraint. Alternatively they could forge their own route, because there's no such thing as a dead end where imagination is concerned.

The result is an inspiring anthology full of ideas, hopes, fears and imagination, proving that creativity really does offer escape, in whatever form you need it.

We encourage young writers to express themselves and address topics that matter to them, which sometimes means exploring sensitive or difficult topics. If you have been affected by any issues raised in this book, details on where to find help can be found at: **www.youngwriters.co.uk/support.**

CONTENTS

Lyndon School, Solihull

Katie Dodd (14)	69
Ben Palmer (13)	70
Emily Wright (11)	71
Theo Hutchinson (11)	72
Evan James Spencer (11)	73
Charlotte Simpson (13)	74
Amber Olivia Lilley Phillips (13)	75
Katie Barber (13)	76
Bisma Bibi (13)	77
Layla Bulaleh (11)	78
Darnell Yesufu (11)	79
Alfie Harwood (11)	80
Tia Ajimal (11)	81
Afnan Omer (11)	82
Aleena Saleem (11)	83
Liam John Clifford (12)	84
Hannah Meaking (12)	85
Callum Doherty (11)	86
Ella Smith (11)	87
Alyssa Campbell (12)	88
May Shirley (11)	89
Benjamin Powell (12)	90
Rhiya Parmar (13)	91
Millie Samantha Lakin (11)	92
Heshaam Mahmmud (11)	93
Joshua Bibb (13)	94
Amelia Cleverly (11)	95
Danny Morris (11)	96
Isha Amaara (12)	97
Sam Kell (11) & Logan	98
Owen Gallagher (11)	99

St Francis Of Assisi Catholic Technology College, Aldridge

Tamzin Timperley (12)	100
Chloe Birtwistle (12)	102
Erin McIntyre (12)	104
James Wilkinson (11)	106
Poppy Fleming (11)	108
Benita Jaeneke (12)	109
Esther Enuoma (11)	110

Hayden Ho (11)	111
Lily Sarah Quinn (11)	112
Sophie Doocey (13)	113
Charlie Adams (12)	114
Megan Amstrong (11)	116
Harriet Fisher (11)	117
Annie Hattersley (13)	118
Ethan Meers (11)	119
Jessica Munslow (12)	120
Freya Coyne (11)	121
Charlotte Freeth (11)	122
Harry J Bradbury (11)	123
Shantel Odera Dike (11)	124
Millie Anne Kilgallen (13)	125
Elizah-Hannah Haroon (11)	126
Eireann Mae Brannigan (11)	127
Megan Barton (13)	128
Aleksander Graczkowski (11)	129
Matthew John Logan (11)	130
Joel Mulligan (11)	131
Megan Banks (12)	132
Jarlaith Hitchings (11)	133
Violet-May Green (12)	134
Marypeace Osazuwa (11)	135
Katie Martindale (12)	136
Alisha Karunanayake (12)	137
Ruby Wood (12)	138
Serena Nunda (12)	139
Lilly Stone (11)	140
Corben Oakley (12)	141
Oliver Ogbeide (11)	142
Will Mortimer (11)	143

THE POEMS

HOPELESS

Useless cries of pain and misery,
Don't I have the right to my own liberty?
Never-ending abuse of false accusations and violence,
My brain speaks wonders, but my lips stick to silence.
Losing friends with a terrible argument,
Shouting words of harsh judgement.
People stare with utter sympathy,
Leaving me feeling nothing but stupidity.
Lonely days fighting my enemies,
Wishing for the days of serenity.
People say that I am heartless,
As I drift away into my pool of darkness.

Malaika Amin (12)
Abu Bakr Girls' School, Walsall

THE BRUTAL KIDNAPPER

The clouds were a shadowy ghost, filling the sky with misty fear,
The wind warned the world about the deadly event that was going to happen,
And the children's fear came sprinting, sprinting, sprinting,
The children's fear came sprinting up to the abandoned, gloomy mansion...

As he was approaching, he tightened his hold on the children there,
Shrieking, weeping, sobbing, they had nothing to spare,
Threatened and tortured, they were,
Miraculously, the kidnapper was chuckling and laughing his heart out.

He had swollen red blisters on his forehead,
A figure of scars above his chin,
A jacket of a blazing nightmare,
And breeched and crumpled skin.

Leaving the children locked away and scared,
He unfortunately met an undercover cop.
He got caught,
There was fighting, screaming, and wars occurring.

Moments later, the criminal laughed in triumph,
His knee up high,

While the kiddies breathed,
Their last...

Nadirah Begum (11)
Abu Bakr Girls' School, Walsall

A MOTHER'S LOVE!

A mother's love
is something no one can explain.

There are times when
only my mother can understand my pain.

Till the day I get my wings
your support has been in full swing.

You were my first friend
and your love knew no end.

Like a candle
you spread light.

Whenever I'm with you
everything's alright.

My mother loves me
anywhere.

Her everlasting love is
beyond compare!

Hafiza Hussain (11)
Abu Bakr Girls' School, Walsall

THE JOURNEY

From below the sea to the uplifted mountain is where the
journey starts
The connection between the Earth and the heart
Is too endless to be able to find
Unleash the secrets of the world
Wherever it can be found

Not every adventure is the same
Cultures and lifestyles are all unique
Enjoy every sight that you see
Before the journey ends.

Zahraa Ishak (12)
Abu Bakr Girls' School, Walsall

ODE TO MY FUTURE DAUGHTER

Firstly,
Welcome to the world,
I know it's messy, dirty and scary,
But you will change this,
I know you will because you are a shining light,
One of hope and beauty,
One that, if used properly, can change the world,
Stop wars and even start them.

Secondly,
No matter what anyone says, you are beautiful,
You are my little bundle of joy,
I love you with all my heart,
Because you are mine,
Mine to love,
Mine to hold,
Mine to protect,
And mine forever.

Thirdly,
Your first real long-term partner, whether they are your
boyfriend or girlfriend,
They will break your heart - this is inevitable,
But you will survive because you are a survivor,

My advice to you when this happens is:
Eat lots of ice cream,
Then brush yourself off and find someone new,
You have to get through all the frogs,
Before you get your prince or princess.

Fourthly,
You can be whoever or whatever you want,
You can love whomever you want,
You will never, ever receive any judgement from me,
If you want to marry a girl, go for it,
If you want to be a boy, then I will welcome a son,
I never want you to feel scared to tell me anything,
And I mean anything!

Penultimately,
When you have a daughter of your own,
You will understand why I am so protective,
You will understand why I will always say,
Without fail, when you are feeling ugly or not good enough,
That you are perfect and the most beautiful girl I have ever
seen,
You will know why you bring me such joy,
You will know that I would rather die than let you come to
harm,
Not a hair on your head will be touched by evil,
Or a single drop of blood be taken from you.

Lastly,
When I am gone, although that is a long time from now,
I will watch over you, protect you,
And when you are crying because something has made you sad,
I will be there, holding you in my arms,
You are my angel and I love you,
Please don't ever forget that.

Love, your future mum.

Gabriella Wyldbore (14)
Dormston School, Sedgley

WHAT I AM AND CAN BE!

I am a god, peering down on our world.
I am a helping hand, never turning my back.
I am a story to forever be told.
I am an eagle - never seeking prey, but seeking life within.

My mind holds everything in a suitable place.
My mind is that light, so bright, a beam of diamonds.
My mind lives beyond all imagination.
My mind is stronger than God himself.

I am Neptune's rings, colder than ice.
I am the sun's beams that shine down on our life.
I am the moon's reflection, so bright that it could blind you.
I am a heart that remains inside my soul until I come again.

My soul is the everlasting, ever-expanding piece of the
puzzle.
My night is gorgeous, filled with emeralds dazzling brighter
than ever.
My memory remains ancient, but filled with life and love.
My imagination can never be stopped until life takes its
place.

Amy Robinson (11)
Dormston School, Sedgley

I'M FINE

I have a sweet smile,
I promise I do,
But beneath my sweet attitude,
Under all the sweet smiles and happy chats,
Is underlying pain that drives me insane.
I can see it inside my heart, but I try to grin,
It always stays the same every day,
I hide my pain and say I'm fine.
I am a con artist, fooling people into loving a version of me
who does not exist,
I am a hard stone with a cold heart,
If I need an instant smile, it will appear,
But sometimes it crumbles into tears,
I have to muffle the pain,
So I repeat,
"I'm fine."
I try to feel no pain,
I leave myself stains on my broken soul like the dust of
broken coal,
I am lost in this empty world in my mind.
Sirens ring in my ears,
Lights flash across my vision,
A warning to hide and just smile,
I repeat, "I'm fine."

But there is something so small and dim,
It is like a flare from deep within,
It is tiny, so tiny, but saves me from dying underneath my
perfect smile,
It's called love...
Love is such a funny thing,
It can fix broken hearts or break them more.
I used to fear love,
I was worried about people seeing the real me,
The numb mess of that girl they thought I used to be,
So I hide my pain and smile and repeat,
"I'm fine,
I'm fine,
I'm fine..."

Megan Drew (14)
Dormston School, Sedgley

GIFTED

There I was, sat all alone,
Wishing I wasn't on my own,
Then she came, a special gift from the sea,
Somehow I knew she would come and comfort me.
She chirped and chittered and danced and played,
She put a smile on my face for the rest of the day.
She jumped and leapt gracefully in the air,
With love and pride and lots of care.
I started to understand the language she spoke,
She spoke of happiness and freedom with lots of hope.
She said her name was Delphina Amy-Lee,
And she longed to be happy and live her life freely.
Now I know the magic and power we share,
I feel her love and her endless care,
I long to be with her and live the rest of my life happily,
Someday, I will...
I have a dolphin with me.

Rosie Sutton (11)
Dormston School, Sedgley

2009

I was dreaming one night
Of his blonde hair and his blue eyes
I could hear him pacing
Beyond the thin walls of my bedroom
I had no friends till I was thirteen
I was lonely, I was lonely
Then he saved me, and yes, I'm sorry
But I still love you.

Does he remember the time
When we first met, in front of all his friends?
Does he remember the time
When he said that he loved me in the snow?
Does he remember the time
When I kissed him and we were just fine?
Does he remember the time
Back in 2009?

Was he dreaming last night
Of my pale skin under the night sky?
Baby, I miss you, I really do
Oh hun, I still love you.

Layla-Mae Lunn (14)
Dormston School, Sedgley

THE BIG PREP

I call the field home sweet home,
Others call it a war zone.
In the distance, lights flicker,
Walking out to a ticker.
Heading out to the sideline,
Through the tunnel, about to shine.
We all emerge to the crowd,
The supporters very loud.
My brain says, *will our team work?*
The enemies giggle and smirk.
All together we huddle,
Just like a penguin cuddle...

Jessica Potts (13)
Dormston School, Sedgley

CHANGE

The telephone was an object that sat on the table in the hall
you had to turn a dial to make a call.
The TV was a large box with a small black and white screen
there was no remote control to change the channel
you had to get up off your seat and mess with the panel.
It was a shot in the dark, taking photos of family, friends and picturesque scenes
the film had to be developed, not viewed on the screen...
Computers were something of the future
'Wi-Fi' was a funny word you'd never heard of
and 'catch up' was when you were last in a race
you were told to run faster to keep up with the pace.
Cardboard boxes went out of fashion and plastic was introduced
it was everyone's passion.
Nothing escaped a plastic wrapper,
it really made everything look very dapper.
But did they realise the damage it would do?
Not only bags, bottles and wraps,
but things that people flushed down the loo.
Our rivers and oceans are all now affected
and our beautiful wildlife that should be protected
is at risk from the artificial product that this world perfected.

Daniella Lewis (13)
Lady Hawkins' School & Sixth Form, Kington

MUSIC THROUGH THE DECADES

Music through the decades,
Well, where do I begin?
The 1940s taught us how to swing,
With Glenn Miller's 'Chattanooga Choo Choo',
And things I can't begin to tell you.
The 1950s gave us a legend, Elvis Presley.
Doris sang 'Que Sera Sera',
And Chuck sang about a car.
Motown came in the sixties,
With rock 'n' roll and more,
The Beatles wanted to hold your hand,
Before they were sixty-four!
Along came the seventies,
Where disco first began,
Hot Chocolate sang 'Every 1's A Winner', baby,
And you could've been a lady.
The eighties brought us glam rock,
U2 couldn't live 'With or Without You',
And New Order sang about a Monday that was rather blue.
Nirvana shaped the nineties,
Green Day were 'Having a Blast',
And then arrived the noughties,
All Saints sang 'Pure Shores',
And not forgetting Jason Mraz who sang 'I'm Yours'.

And finally, 2010s, the newest of them all,
Where Taylor Swift is having a ball,
And Ed Sheeran is 'Talking Out Loud'.

Sophie Edwards (13)
Lady Hawkins' School & Sixth Form, Kington

HISTORY CANNOT CHANGE

The light crept out from behind the trees,
Though it did not bring any light to his heart,
Sorrow spread through him like a disease,
Desperate to consume him in misery.

The mighty walls lining the entrance,
Now crumbled heaps of rock,
Smothered and strangled by ivy hands,
Iron gates and a new padlock.

He scrambled over the railing,
Wrinkles etched in his face,
In front of him darted a squirrel,
Swiftly sweeping along in haste.

Saw the place a little boy played,
Many years ago in the summer,
Watched him run, not afraid,
Of the dark, gloomy woods by the manor.

Followed him as he skipped and danced,
Along the path to his fairy land,
The sky was blue, the air was clear,
And the midsummer breeze cooled the atmosphere.

Colossal columns of smooth grey stone,
Outlining the grand entrance,
Leaping through the door,
The boy disappeared without a glance.

A hollow space in the lonely estate,
Demolished long ago,
Time made it this way,
History cannot change,
The mistakes that we undergo.

Tessa Westlake (12)
Lady Hawkins' School & Sixth Form, Kington

FOUR SEASONS

Snow is falling on a cold winter's day,
It's a crisp winter's evening and the log burner is glowing,
Icicles are hanging from the windowsill,
It's dark outside as the cold wind blows,
Unwrapping Christmas presents from underneath the
Christmas tree,
The snow begins to fall on the cold winter's day.

It's the first day of spring,
Trees grow and rivers flow,
Winter footprints are in the past,
The grass is green across the hills,
But yellow bloom the daffodils,
Mellow, mild, May Day, calling children out to play.

Woods full of blueberries and hedges full of blooms,
Opening the windows to let in some air,
Ice-cold drinks wait for us in the fridge,
Night of summer stars shine above,
How beautiful the rain after the heat of the day.

The leaves are falling,
Colourful they fall,
Seasons of mist, mellow and fruitful,
Fields full of pumpkins as the full moon shimmers on them,
Halloween has come with all the spooky creatures,
To scare away the horrible teachers.

Alivia Wheeler (12)
Lady Hawkins' School & Sixth Form, Kington

THE CHALLENGE OF CHANGES

Mirrors don't change your appearance, they change the heart.
You may not be able to see it, but it is there
Protect your good image from the eyes of haters
Mirrors just prove your beauty
The reflection doesn't show who you really are
Appearance shouldn't be a battle, don't let it be.

The environmental changes just prove how strong we are together,
Littering is a way of showing disrespect to the world.
Earth provides enough to satisfy every man's need, but not every man's greed.
Create a comforting surrounding for new life
Be proud of the world we live in
Attack for the world with faith and positivity.

The most important thing in the world is family and love.
Remember, the world picked your loved ones,
Family isn't just important, it is everything!
The love of family is the world's greatest blessing,
Family is the world's masterpiece.
Your appearance, attitude and confidence define you as a person.

Charlotte Priday (11)
Lady Hawkins' School & Sixth Form, Kington

A CHANGE

A change of time, a time or place,
A change of life, a change of pace.

A change can be good, a change can be bad,
A change can be happy, a change can be sad.

A change of towns, a change of schools,
Life can always change the rules.

A change of Dad, change of Mum,
All the fun has just begun.

A change of name, a change of age,
A change of sex, let's turn the page.

A change of warmth, a change of strength,
A change of weather, a change of length.

A change of love, a change of life,
A change of family, a change of size.

A change of season, a change of holiday,
A change of house, a change of history.

A change of colour, a change of clothes,
A change of make-up, a change of shoes.

A change of presents, a change of Easter eggs,
A change of birthdays, a change of friends.

If at first you hate the change, look back
Look back on it.
In the future, I'm sure you'll regret it.

Alexa Bounds (13)
Lady Hawkins' School & Sixth Form, Kington

CHANGE OF SEASONS

Winter
The foggy blue skies against the bright white clouds
Crashing as the weather turns down
In the night, a frost freezes
Pick an ice cup up, but
It's so clear like a crystal
Hurry up, otherwise it will tear!

Summer
Bright, hot, clear blue skies
Shining down on the bright green grass
Children sunbathing - wait, don't get too tanned
Play out in the sun, just don't get burnt
It's starting to get chilly now, so hurry up and enjoy the sun!

Autumn
Massive, brown, empty trees
Crumpled up green leaves
Scattered against the cold floor
Uncrumpling, turning very brown
Wind blowing colourful leaves, swishing around.

Spring
Lighter blue skies, misty clouds amongst the bright blue sea
Plants are slowly drowning in the damp, soggy ground
As we watch whilst we are snuggled up

Our warm hot chocolate is the only thing keeping us warm
As we watch the time fly past us as we sleep.

Kayleigh Wood (11)
Lady Hawkins' School & Sixth Form, Kington

SEASONS OF THE YEAR

Snowdrops are a sign of spring,
Winter trees start recovering,
New green leaves are growing.

Pretty pink blossom has come,
Clouds have gone,
You are able to see the sun.

In summer, it is never grey,
Most people go on holiday,
Brighter now and longer days.

Flowers open up in summer,
The weather forecast shows signs of thunder,
Thanks to flies, the animals suffer.

Heaps of leaves begin to spread,
Since it's the beginning of fall.

Halloween has come much closer,
All the shops are changing over,
The nights not getting warmer.

In December, it is really icy,
All the shops are getting pricy,
All over the place is holly and ivy.

First time this winter, it's snowing,
All the Christmas lights are glowing,
Children are wishing and hoping,
Parents are barely coping!

The end of winter, nearly spring,
Time for a new year to begin!

Millie May Goodwin (12)
Lady Hawkins' School & Sixth Form, Kington

WILL I WIN?

I jumped out the Battle Bus, hoping for the win
I land at Tilted and that went down the bin.
I played and played, landing Retail and Salty
But in my first chest, I found a bolty.
I rushed a default and shot him in the head
But thirty seconds later, I was dead.
I got to top ten, but that wasn't enough
I fell down a hill and that made me bluff.
My friends called me trash and said to delete the game
Because 'I don't know how to aim'.
I switched to Builder Pro to see how it would go
But I didn't realise my sensitivity was low.
There was one person left, I thought I was the best
But in the end, I was just like the rest.
I started using SMG
Every day, skipping my tea.
I was getting better and better
At my door arrived a letter.
I was invited to PAX West
Now I know I'm the best.

Thomas Howells (13)
Lady Hawkins' School & Sixth Form, Kington

PRIDE POEM

It used to be looked down on if you were gay
You would receive floods of hate
And in some places around the world, it's something you
could be killed for
It was something people were ashamed of
Scared to come out and express their feelings

Although still in modern day society, some people protest
against LGBTQ+ rights
People still use the word 'gay' as an insult towards other
people
Some people are still scared to come out
From fear of people's reactions that are so important to
them
In some places, gay marriage is still illegal

But people are waking up
We are all waking up
Festivals are held to support the community
Places around the world are legalising gay marriage
Many more people are able to feel safe with their sexuality
Society is changing and finally accepting us all as equals.

Myrna Phyllis Smith (12)
Lady Hawkins' School & Sixth Form, Kington

CHANGE

Seasons come and seasons go
the changing colours are a beautiful show.
Yellows, greens, reds and golds
watching nature all unfold.

Spring welcomes the season of birth
flowers burst and blossom from the earth.
New animals hopping around
wherever you look, new life can be found.

Summer skies are so bright
longer days and shorter nights.
Playing on the beach is so fun
eating ice cream in the sun.

Autumn, the leaves begin to fall
the trees are bare and yet stand so tall.
The wind is howling around the land
the fireworks display is so grand.

Winter frost on the ground
icicles hanging all around.
Christmas is coming and a new year
with celebrations and a cheer.

Seasons come and seasons go
which is your favourite?
I don't know!

Elizabeth Woods (12)
Lady Hawkins' School & Sixth Form, Kington

CHANGE

Winter is cold, get some warm clothes
you will need to get prepared
better start shopping before the stores run out
get stocked up on tea and coffee
and clothes that are warm and fluffy
the snow is about to come
get your spades at the ready!

Spring is ready
the flowers are bloomy
get ready for the sun to come
if you get hay fever, better get some tablets
this year is going to be a good one
the animals are coming
there are lambs and chicks that are going to be running and
hopping
having a good time.

Summer is here, the sun is shining
heating and boiling
the rain is going, get ready for water fights
get the barbecue out
invite friends and family to have a party
get the ice cream and prepare the icy cool drinks
summer's here again!

Harry Griffiths (12)
Lady Hawkins' School & Sixth Form, Kington

TECH IS AWESOME

Technology has changed a lot
From a floppy disc to a laptop and whatnot
You cook food with tech, like a microwave oven
You drive tech, like a Ford Focus or Land Rover
You can play with tech, like a PS4 or you can Xbox
You can watch Emmerdale or Coronation Street with tech like a TV or phone
You can tell the time with tech, like a watch or an alarm clock
Tech helps you get up in the morning gloom
It helps you get out of your bedroom
Tech can do work for you, like robots building cars, exploring Mars, driving self-driving cars
You can communicate with a telecommunication device
You can teach with tech's interactive boards, Bitesize
You can pay with tech, club cars, bank cards, gift cards, credit cards
You can party with tech's music, CDs, DVDs, DJs, radio, mics.

Oliver Copeland (12)
Lady Hawkins' School & Sixth Form, Kington

THE NEXT STEP

I awoke in the morning,
my heart pounding,
my mind full of curiosity,
I said to myself, "Is this really happening?"
I took one look at my uniform all neatly hung up,
this was a big change.

I closed the door, then it came to me,
my stomach felt like it had disappeared,
I slowly took one step,
I was finally ready for this,
I checked I had got everything for that day,
this was a big change.

I got off at the school and I was really excited,
there were people in my year that I'd never met before.
In five years' time, these would be my friends for life.
We all met in the hall after the long holiday,
and played some games to get to know each other.
This was a big change.

Seren Price (11)
Lady Hawkins' School & Sixth Form, Kington

CHANGE

Death, upgrades, weather, new life, new house,
Everything must change,
From the smallest atom
To the tallest tree.
Plants and animals,
Pulled by death,
Every hour, day, week, month and year.
Anything could change at any time,
Buildings could collapse,
Wars could start,
Crops could die.
Every day we face change in all different ways.
Today or tomorrow it could happen,
Even at night.
Ordinary things could change
Every day this year, next year, any year,
It could happen at any time.
People you know could move away
And be forgotten
And lost in memory.
Empires may fall and people will die
Seasons will change and years will go by.
Everything must change one day.

Wesley Squire (13)
Lady Hawkins' School & Sixth Form, Kington

TECHNOLOGY

Technology is changing the world,
You can now leave the world in VR,
The cars now run on technology,
Soon, they will drive themselves.
Those are good changes, here are some bad:
People can access your private information if you're not careful,
Some take to technology to be happy and without it they are miserable,
Don't forget artificial intelligence that is smarter than humans,
The world is controlled by the Internet, without it we would be nothing.
Let's go back to some good things,
You can text or email someone from across the world with some buttons,
People make a living out of the internet,
Some on YouTube, Instagram and Twitter,
Even inspire their viewers or followers.

Cameron Cutt (12)
Lady Hawkins' School & Sixth Form, Kington

CHANGE OF THE SEASONS

The seasons have big changes.
Spring is cold and misty,
and it has white, fluffy clouds,
and it is lighter when it is later in the night.

However, summer is warmer,
bright yellow sun,
steamy, bright and really light,
when it is later, you can play with family and friends,
without worrying about it raining.

Autumn is when the leaves fall off the trees,
when they fall, it looks fantastic and it's amusing to watch
it.
It gets cold very easily,
however, it gets darker earlier in the day,
and there are fluffy, white, snowy-looking clouds.

Winter is very cold.
In the distance of a cold day, there will be mist.
It is extremely cloudy in winter.

Taylor Davies (11)
Lady Hawkins' School & Sixth Form, Kington

CHANGES IN WEATHER

Spring is cold and frosty,
the animals and creatures begin to snuggle in,
whilst the grass starts to grow.

Summer is warm and cosy,
the sun is always bright,
with lots of trips to the freezer to keep you alive,
as you lie in the fresh green grass.

Autumn is when the crispy leaves start to decrease,
and all the evenings turn dark rather than bright,
and the best thing about this season is definitely Bonfire
Night!

Winter is always frosty and cold,
the days turn short and the nights turn long,
often, it will snow,
a good time to go sledging and skiing,
as long as you don't fall off your sledge,
make sure that you have loads of exciting fun.

Hayden James (11)
Lady Hawkins' School & Sixth Form, Kington

SOCIAL MEDIA

There was a time of not pretending,
A hug could break down a wall, a simple first date.
Didn't matter how glamorous our lives were.
Social media has changed; it has changed how we see each
other and how we value ourselves.
Before, people didn't care about their appearances.
Now, 'what will they think of me?' will be the first question.
Everything we do is a story for others to read and comment
on.
Every picture comes with a package,
Put a filter on it, no one will notice,
Making sure it gets likes and comments.
Behind a picture is an untold story.
One hundred pictures were taken, each one denied until
they find the right one.
The caption does the lying...

Amy Rose Veary (13)
Lady Hawkins' School & Sixth Form, Kington

CHANGE

Technology has changed the world,
In the olden days, they had no tech,
Instead, they went down to the rec,
But now, we just stay inside,
Playing on video games and texting friends,
Normally, we don't do a lot,
We don't get fit,
All we do is wiggle our thumbs,
And wield our controllers as if they were swords,
Yelling down all the way from upstairs,
"Get off the Internet down there!"
Then your angry mum and dad come stomping up the stairs,
Shouting at you to turn it off,
You say goodbye to all your friends,
You press the button to turn it off,
Jumping into bed, waiting for the morning to come,
To play the game you treasure the most.

William Goode (12)
Lady Hawkins' School & Sixth Form, Kington

STORY OF CHANGE

When your hair becomes thin and grey
and wrinkles take your face
this is a sign of ageing.
But you will find your place.
"There is light at the end of the tunnel, my friend."
You will be here again.

When the rock comes tumbling downwards
and the world is burning bright
this is a sign of destruction.
But refuge will be found.
"There is light at the end of the tunnel, my dear."
Here you are again.

When your heart is old and weak
and you stumble on your feet
this is a sign of your passing.
But don't give up right now.
"There is light at the end of the tunnel, my world."
That is where you'll be.

Toby Lloyd (11)
Lady Hawkins' School & Sixth Form, Kington

THE JOURNEY OF LIFE

One of my first memories
is from when I was three
my parents split up
my mum had no backup
she moved far away
and found a place to stay
with her family
she thought it was a fantasy

My mum moved to a town
and was on the countdown
Vicky had two kids
but still no time to close her eyelids
then she met a man
with a builder's van
his name was David
and Mum's worries faded

They had a son
and we had a lot of fun
his name is Oliver
but his nickname's Mijolivers
a marriage made in heaven
though they hadn't been to Devon
and, anyhow
that brings us up to now!

Charlie Ray (11)
Lady Hawkins' School & Sixth Form, Kington

TECHNOLOGY

The world is evolving
So is the other world
The world of technology
Where your data is stored
Or you're texting your family in-law
But not all is good
We have additions to these things, let me mention a few
YouTube and Netflix, Twitch and its streamers,
And many games including Fortnite.
Don't forget VR gaming where you can go on a nice trip.
On Facebook, you must be careful
As Mark Zuckerberg could be stealing your data and selling
it to government organisations!
Maybe he could be watching your private conversations.
But put that aside
Because technology can also save lives
And it could save yours...

Jack Ellsmore (11)
Lady Hawkins' School & Sixth Form, Kington

THE SEASON TREE

New curls of growth unfurl as winter makes way for spring.
Shades of green, so fresh and full of promise,
Brighten the view from my window.

Glorious bunches of blossom hang heavy as spring makes
way for summer,
Heady scents, blooms of candy pink,
Brighten the view from my window.

The leaves are falling, crunchy and withered as summer
makes way for autumn.
Tumbling wisps of ochre, chestnut and crimson,
Brighten the view from my window.

Icicle diamonds hang from skeleton branches as autumn
makes way for winter.
Shades of white, iridescent and dazzling,
Brighten the view from my window.

Jace Guy (12)
Lady Hawkins' School & Sixth Form, Kington

THE BATTLE OF CHANGE

As the seasons move,
as you age and become wrinkly,
you have to adapt to your new life.
Though your eyes may be blinded by your thoughts,
let your heart, not your brain, control your choice.
As new battles begin and old ones end,
you will always have a challenge to mend.
No matter your height or your shape,
you're the one living in you, so don't let others define you,
'cause you are the one who chose this life.
If you're happy, why should others change you?
When you are scared in the dark,
it is up to you to find the light,
that makes you shine so bright.

Naomy Taralunga (12)
Lady Hawkins' School & Sixth Form, Kington

CHANGE

Change happens there and here
Change happens in England and Spain
Change happens to bugs and beasts from everywhere
Change is as simple as sun and moon
Change is the movement from night to day
Change can be a different holiday location
Change can be using a different pen or pencil
Change forms friendships and love
Change is not knowing something, to knowing something
Change can create hard or simple decisions
Change can trail through spring and summer
Change can be growing your hair long or cutting your hair
short
Change can be for the better or for the worst.

Grace Dinsdale (12)
Lady Hawkins' School & Sixth Form, Kington

POEM ABOUT CHANGE

A change in time, a change in place
A change in school, a change in job
A change in home, a change in lifestyle
Whatever the change, you can adapt
To bring on more opportunities and chances

Change is the change to perfection
Change is the change of mindset
Change is the change of a way of life
Change is the challenges you put yourself through
Change is taking a step into the unknown

Change comes and goes with the seasons
Change can always be lurking around the corner
Change can make or break something
Change can be good or bad.

Charlie Harris (13)
Lady Hawkins' School & Sixth Form, Kington

BUTTERFLY

We are like caterpillars,
We both have legs,
We have babies,
Though they lay eggs.

And we can speak,
Can they too?
That decision is up to you.

When we die, it's not the end,
But just the beginning, I shall defend,
Our coffin is our chrysalis,
Strong and hollow,
But a special gift is soon to follow,
We come out of the coffin,
Bright and strong,
As a beautiful butterfly all along.

So when someone dies,
Just stop and think,
They're flapping their wings,
With every blink.

Violet Redfern (12)
Lady Hawkins' School & Sixth Form, Kington

CHANGES

The world is always changing
Nothing stays the same
Cars are smaller, quieter and better for us
Phones are no longer just to call
They are windows to our world
Food is wonkier, no longer a need for perfection

It's okay to be sad and say it out loud
Now there's a friendly ear to listen
Sadly, it's not all good in the world
Guns and knives rule our streets
The need to be bigger and better takes over minds
Let's hope the future becomes nicer to be in
Full of love and laughter
Less hate and misery.

Mya Griffiths (12)
Lady Hawkins' School & Sixth Form, Kington

CHANGE

Change can be good and it can be bad,
Like changes in weather.
When it's winter, it's cold, snowy and wet most of the time.
Winter's wet, sloppy and brown mud.
It changes from winter to summer.

Spring is cold and crunchy underfoot,
Spring has green leaves as they flow slowly down from the
tree,
With the young birds whistling for food,
And swallows soaring in the sky.

Summer's golden sun as it gleams down on the world,
Cars glisten as the bright sun burns,
It is fun when you play with friends.

Rhys James Dickerson (11)
Lady Hawkins' School & Sixth Form, Kington

DEATH

He was here in my room,
Waiting for the moment of doom.
Ready to take my life away,
Death had come to this day.
It was a horrible, dark ghost,
I was waiting for it like the post.
This felt like it was my last hour,
The time I'd lose my mind and power.
His deathly sound stalking me,
I knew it was meant to be.
Jump off a bridge was what I wanted to do,
I thought it would've been best, it's true.
Because of this ghost, I would end up in a grave,
My life would end,
No more family, no more friends...

Samuel Garibbo (12)
Lady Hawkins' School & Sixth Form, Kington

CHANGING SEASONS

Spring is cold and crisp
And all things start to grow
The birds begin to make nests
And the lawn will need a mow

Summer is bright and warm
The days are long and fun
With many trips to the seaside
Frolicking in the sun

Autumn is when the leaves fall
And all the evenings aren't light
We all go trick or treating
But the best fun is Bonfire Night

Winter can sometimes be bleak
If we are lucky, it will be snowy
It's exciting to all go sledging
But not if it's too blowy.

Jacob Hazelman (11)
Lady Hawkins' School & Sixth Form, Kington

CHANGES TO AUTUMN TO WINTER

Clocks go back again
Nights are darker
Autumn is the first cold season after summer
The leaves start to turn yellow and orange
They start to fall off the trees
Animals hibernating
More people stay inside with the duvet over them
Gets colder and colder and then it turns to winter
Fires and heaters in homes start getting used again
Guy Fawkes gets burned again
Children start collecting conkers
Advent calendars get opened
People sit in front of the fire and drink hot chocolate
With marshmallows and cream.

Zoe Jones (13)
Lady Hawkins' School & Sixth Form, Kington

MOVING SCHOOL

Moving school means leaving your friends,
It means your friends are sad,
It means you're leaving,
It means you are withering up like a dying leaf,
It brings broken friendship circles.

Moving school means starting new,
It means making new friends,
It means making a good impression,
It brings happiness,
It brings bliss.

Moving school means leaving your friends,
But it means making a good impression.
It means your leaving,
But can bring happiness.

Moving school is brilliant!

Aurora Celeste Dean (12)
Lady Hawkins' School & Sixth Form, Kington

A CHAPTER OF LIFE

I was like a roller coaster, up and down,
my feelings were hurt,
and I didn't make a sound.

I needed to make a change to be me,
to be happy again, and
to start to believe.

I made a change and I was glad,
and I was no longer that roller coaster,
always being sad.

My anger was gone and I decided to move on,
it was time to say goodbye,
and leave the bullies behind.

I'm now on this path that is just for me,
it's smooth, not bumpy and,
no drama's around me!

Freya Harris (13)
Lady Hawkins' School & Sixth Form, Kington

FOUR SEASONS
CHANGING

As one season rolls into another
The trees go from brown to white to green
Always going around in an infinite circle
Winter covering the surroundings in snow
Making everybody happy
Spring, the wind blows, the trees grow
As the flowers grow up to make the world beautiful
Summer, the sun shines as children run around
And animals come out to play
Then go back into hiding
As autumn starts, the trees go brown
The leaves fall and get ready for winter
As the cycle of life carries on
As if there is no end.

Arran Phillips (12)
Lady Hawkins' School & Sixth Form, Kington

THE HUMAN PALETTE

Black and white
Yellow and brown
Colours of the palette
Beautiful colours
These words have a meaning
But if I try to paint a picture with these colours
It would be more than just a painting
Unlike paints
People do not mix as easily
As the artist's palette.
We are made to mix together
Who knew,
That a colour could create so much misery?
But history has proved to us that we
The human colour palette
Can separate like oil and water
If only we were solvent.

Ashley Stockton Hemuss (13)
Lady Hawkins' School & Sixth Form, Kington

AGE

One day you're young,
One day you're old,
But remember the truth,
Your brain is very bold.
With ideas better than theirs,
That spark your brain,
Your lives are not the same.

Beware, you're precious!
Take care,
As you start to grow your first hair.
You weep in joy,
Waiting to change,
To your final stage.
You're staring at life,
Loving every second,
To sleep with memories,
And wait for your time to end.

Hannah Victoria Smith (12)
Lady Hawkins' School & Sixth Form, Kington

HEARTS

This is to my parents
From the only child
Of the family made of
Three.

It's been a long four years,
I've cried a thousand tears,
And all I've heard are slamming doors,
But now we're here after the war.

Your love was broken up by
Shattered hearts.

Change can be for the best
Of for the worst,
This was for the
Best.

Therefore, I'm not pretending when I say,
Change fixed my heart...

Saoirse Brealey (12)

Lady Hawkins' School & Sixth Form, Kington

58

CHANGE

Moving is a strange thing,
Moving house, moving school,
No friends, different place,
Those are negative things about moving!

Did not know,
Where my future would begin,
Stuck inside,
All lonely.

Until I went to LHS,
Found a few friends,
Knew my way around,
Got to class on time.

Now, overall, I've changed,
Everyone is really wonderful and generous,
I never want to leave LHS,
Only when my time comes.

Sophie Matthews (11)
Lady Hawkins' School & Sixth Form, Kington

CHANGE

Not K3 is my name
And I have over 400 wins
I'm the best in Kington
So bow down to me
If you play with me, you can see
My average kills are 33.

There's one person left
And they're scared of me
It's as if I'm getting kills for free
Why don't you just look at me?
I'm better than Tfue, you will see
I will shoot you in the head
Whilst I'm eating my tea
Just wait and see.

Harry Rollings (12)
Lady Hawkins' School & Sixth Form, Kington

FOR THE BAD AND THE GOOD

Technology
how it has changed
for the best
or the worst.
Nuclear bombs
and hospital tech.
This technology kills
and destroys us
at the same time.
One man is paralysed
by the aftershock
of a nuclear blast.
He is rushed to the
tech-filled hospital.
His life is saved by a machine
that helps heal his back vertebrae
and stops his back crushing his lungs.

Diggory Rayment (13)
Lady Hawkins' School & Sixth Form, Kington

A NEW DAY

Misty, damp, cold and crisp
Dropped leaves underfoot
Colours of autumn
Browns, yellows, reds and oranges
Air smells fresh
A sheep bleats on the hill
The red sun begins to rise
Warm light on the apple tree
The sky turning bright blue
With fluffy white clouds
Dotted about
Early birds singing
And the hedgehog crawls through the red and orange
leaves
A new day begins.

Eva Cooley (12)
Lady Hawkins' School & Sixth Form, Kington

CHANGE

It's misty in the morning
it changes so fast
from cold to hot
from misty to not
every hour
you see a glimmer
the cracks in the clouds
growing fatter and slimmer
light cascading through
slowly dazzling
incandescently melting
the chill to a positive degree
throughout the day
misty to light transmutation
slowly to dark as it reverts
back to the start.

Maximus Roberts (12)
Lady Hawkins' School & Sixth Form, Kington

CHANGE

When we get older
Some of us get balder
Then we have a head
As smooth as an egg
Some of us get taller
Some of us get smaller
We can go on to do big things
You just need to believe
Then you will achieve
We start our journey in spring
And have fun through the year
Then our journey ends in summer
We all go on a special journey
So let's take it together.

Katie Newton (12)
Lady Hawkins' School & Sixth Form, Kington

GONE

As quick as a shot from a gun
He vanished from our lives
A distant memory
Never seen again
Gone

No more racing around like a rocket on four legs
No more stroking him
No more feeding him
No more playing with him
Gone

Haunting our minds
Absent from our lives
Disappeared forever
Our lives changed, now he's
Gone.

Edith Annie Goodwin (11)
Lady Hawkins' School & Sixth Form, Kington

CHANGE

Young men fought,
Boys followed,
War broke out,
Women worked,
Farmed the land,
Children giving a helping hand,
Innocent lives taken,
Civil blood was spilt,
Men died in vain,
Men were killed,
Woman grieved,
War stopped,
Peace arose,
Silence emerged.
Change...

Carys McAlpine (12)
Lady Hawkins' School & Sixth Form, Kington

AUTUMN

Green, gold, red, brown,
The change in leaves all around,
Autumn coming and going.

Days drawing in,
Fires lit,
Pumpkins being carved.

Poppies pinned on clothes,
Remembering those who fought for us.

Green, gold, red, brown,
Autumn!

Lily Price (12)
Lady Hawkins' School & Sixth Form, Kington

CHANGES

M y life has been a mix of changes
Y ou may not understand

L iving with different people
I n my life of movement
F inding the perfect home
E nding up in Kington when I was three.

Sophie Pochin (11)
Lady Hawkins' School & Sixth Form, Kington

MASKS

A fake, phony smiling face,
Concealed feelings of utter disgrace.
Feelings of humiliation and shame in what she did,
Feelings of embarrassment were what she hid.

A speech about peace she used to hide,
A bitter, raging fire inside;
Fueled on emotions of fury and vexation,
On the outside, she defused a violent situation.

An angry outburst tried to conceal her blue soul,
Inside feeling as empty as an endless hole.
Her heart was weighed down with severe depression;
She tried to hide it with a storm of aggression.

A thick layer of make-up she claimed hid her impurities,
She wore to hide her insecurities.
Insecurities that made her feel angry and upset,
Hidden by the contents in her make-up set.

Every day a different disguise,
Whether to hide a heavy heart or a belly of butterflies.
Every day, struggling with everyday tasks;
To hide her true feelings, she wore masks.

Katie Dodd (14)
Lyndon School, Solihull

DEAR THERESA MAY

What's the point of Brexit?
Why do we need to exit?

What are you doing, Theresa May?
You're just wasting your day!

You're still trying to make a deal,
Whatever happens, it won't be a steal!

Why has this been discussed for so long?
Did they not think that this might be wrong?

I think we need a new Prime Minister,
Hopefully then, they won't be so sinister.

We might need a different visa,
We might not get very much pizza.

Even if people wanted you to stop,
You'd ignore their opinions and let their spirits drop!

If there was a re-vote,
You'd be grabbing your coat.

You'd be out the door,
With Brexit no more!

Ben Palmer (13)
Lyndon School, Solihull

WORLD WAR SCREAM

There was a day in the past,
A day that all people regret,
It was a day of death, depression and all things you would regret!
The innocent people screaming for help.
No one could help, oh, how they felt...
The bombs, the bodies, scattered everywhere,
Just remembering that time makes me flinch!
I imagine how the soldiers felt back then,
Brave, united,
But inside, they were scared,
As the Spitfire zoomed by, the Messerschmitt flew high,
Bam! Bam! The bombs were dropped!
There was nothing to do but scream and shout,
As the people watched their houses fall down...
I suddenly remember this is all in my head,
As I remember my grandad who is dead...

Emily Wright (11)
Lyndon School, Solihull

THE ROOM OF CHAOS!

Bang!
The gargantuan door slammed,
Instant regret filled my mind,
Ear-piercing screams of terror ricocheted around the room.

"This is the end," whispered a mysterious voice,
A thunderstorm of blood feel from complete obscurity,
I would never dare to fight back,
My intimidated heart began to beat at a thousand miles per hour, and vibrated my whole body.

The next room opened,
There was a jungle of coffins,
Open coffins...
My ears rang loudly.

I heard footsteps that were breathtaking and powerful,
They were not from me.
Who was it?
Could it be the swift shadow who drastically turns my dreams upside down?...

Theo Hutchinson (11)
Lyndon School, Solihull

MY LOVELY DOG

Scamp, you're one of the best and cutest dogs I've ever had!
I love it when I get back from school, because you're always waiting for me
so we can play together on the carpet.
When we play together, I find it so cute when you dance
and also when you wiggle your small tail.
You are so fluffy
also, I love to stroke your back.
I'm so happy I've got you as a dog
I hope that you will last forever
so we can go on a journey when I'm old.
I can't wait to get back home
so I can play with you.

I love you, Scamp
and I know you love me too!

Evan James Spencer (11)
Lyndon School, Solihull

I WILL NEVER UNDERSTAND THE POINT OF FOOTBALL

I will never understand the point of football,
Players crying, rolling around on the floor,
Players acting like babies,
Players diving like Tom Daley.

I will never understand the point of football,
Supporters paying loads of money,
Supporters screaming as loud as lions,
Supporters leaving early to skip the traffic.

I will never understand the point of football,
Players being paid millions,
Players speeding and cheating fines,
Nurses underpaid and overworked, keeping people alive.

I will never understand the point of football.

Charlotte Simpson (13)
Lyndon School, Solihull

CHANGE - A HOMELESS DREAM

My head full of despair
Oh, why is my life so unfair?

My heart full of hope
How grateful I would be
To just have some pennies with me

My life going downhill
It isn't a new thing for me
My energy is low
It's like I'm frozen from within

My brain doesn't function
Like it used to
I don't function without you!

How, oh how did I get this way?
I question that every day

I know I can do this,
I know I can change,
I just have to take a step
Day by day.

Amber Olivia Lilley Phillips (13)
Lyndon School, Solihull

IF I WAS GONE

My hands shaking with panic and stress,
Feet tapping, blood pumping,
A waterfall drains out of my eyes,
Lungs deprived of air, needing to breathe,
My chest is deflating.

A consistent dread weighing me down,
Am I good enough? Will I ever get through this?
My mind's walls closing in on me.
I'm alone. I have no one to talk to.
No one cares.

Anxiety rushing over me,
Forcing tears to fall.
Dread flushing my skin,
A constant fear of failure.

Maybe it would be better if I was gone...

Katie Barber (13)
Lyndon School, Solihull

MY FEELINGS

I am dull and dark
I am left with deep scars and marks
My mind is exploding with pain
Will I feel okay again?
I am scared to go to school
My friends laugh at me like I am a fool
Suffering each night
Thinking that they're always right
Bursting out with tears
I can't show my fears
I had enough of this
Happy, joyful days I miss
Screaming and shouting alone
Because my 'friends' send mean messages on my phone
Why me?
I am the odd one out
No more fake friends
This is the end.

Bisma Bibi (13)
Lyndon School, Solihull

NATURE

For many, its leaves are changing.
For many, its bark is burning,
Rotting every second,
Dying. Will it happen?

For many, there's water draining,
For many, the plastic's filling,
Sinking every second,
Dying. Will it happen?

For many, land is cracking,
For many, land's descending,
Vanishing every second,
Dying. Will it happen?

Where is nature going?
Its downfall at our expense,
With construction and our touring,
Why don't we respect nature?

Layla Bulaleh (11)
Lyndon School, Solihull

THE FUTURE

Have you ever wondered what the future will be like?
What it'll bring?
What you will look like?
What you'll be doing?

Maybe there might be a new flexible phone,
But you never know, you might be working as an
accountant,
Or maybe you'll work in Select & Save!

So many things could happen!
Happy things and sad things could happen,
Deaths, births, successes and failures.
You could be rich or poor!
It's the future - you'll have to wait!

Darnell Yesufu (11)
Lyndon School, Solihull

AN ODE TO MY DOG, MISSY

Missy, my wonderful, beautiful and careful dog.
You are the best thing that ever happened to me.
You comfort me when I'm sad.
You lick me with your warm tongue.
Your fur is as soft as silk.
When we play, you wag your tail as fast as thunder.
You always lie down in bed, chilling and relaxing, waiting for your food and water.
When I lie down, you always headbutt me.
When I play in the pool, you always bark at me.
When you're wet, you get me wet too!
Missy, I love you!

Alfie Harwood (11)
Lyndon School, Solihull

THE WORLD AROUND US!

The world around us is changing,
becoming different every day,
the days are getting warmer,
and the snow starts to melt.

The world around us is dying,
weaker and weaker it becomes,
it can no longer take the pain,
that we have done!

The world around us is crying,
weeping out for help,
the water is evaporating,
as the lands begin to yelp.

Can we change our ways,
or will the world be suffering for more days?

Tia Ajimal (11)
Lyndon School, Solihull

REGRETS

To kill with a knife, no value for life,
To destroy and create sadness.
In a moment of madness,
Blood on your hands,
Ice in your heart,
Any regrets?
Why did it start?

You sit in your cell as your life goes on,
But think of all the families...
Can they be strong?

Every day that passes,
Such emptiness in their hearts,
For the loved ones they lost,
So many questions to be asked.

Afnan Omer (11)
Lyndon School, Solihull

THE MAZE

The leafy-green tangled mess
Was curiously making me say yes
In I go
But I do not know
Heart racing at the speed of light
While I travelled deeper into the night
Dead ends, twists and turns
The raging fire in my lungs burns
Salty tears drop from my throbbing eyes
As the brightness of my torch dies
This was it
The end for me
Bit by bit
There was no key.

Aleena Saleem (11)
Lyndon School, Solihull

THE FUTURE

I lie in my bed
Thinking ahead

What will the world be
In 2023?

Will I be rich? Will I be poor?
When will I find out all of the laws?

Will the Earth still be like this?
Or will an asteroid hit or miss?

Will I get a job?
Or maybe a bigger gob?

Will I be early? Will I be late?
I don't know, I'll just leave it up to fate!

Liam John Clifford (12)
Lyndon School, Solihull

WHAT IS LOVE?

Love is a confusing wonder
Even though I'm depressed down under
Wishing I knew
I just don't know what to do
My head is spinning
I'm just never winning

Feeling like I need to give up
Love is the only one keeping me up
Dying inside, I don't know what's happening
He is my last hope
I've just stopped breathing...

Hannah Meaking (12)
Lyndon School, Solihull

AN ODE TO THE MOON

An ode to the moon,
You should admire her soon,

She's like a natural light,
And she doesn't put up a fight,

She's made of rocks, but that doesn't mean she has a stone heart,
She's as sweet as a tart,

She orbits around the Earth,
She has a big girth,

She makes my night,
She's so bright.

Callum Doherty (11)
Lyndon School, Solihull

AN ODE ABOUT MY DOG

Your eyes shine bright in the moonlight.
Your fur is like a fluffy cloud keeping me so comfy.
Even if you always sleep, I still will give you a treat.
Even if you still sleep at night, you come check up on us at broad daylight.
When I come back from school, I know you're ready to play.
You jump so high, you look like a kangaroo when you bark-a-roo!

Ella Smith (11)
Lyndon School, Solihull

THE GREYHOUND

Small paws
Long tail
Compared to a
Cheetah's tail
Long nose
Pointy ears
A bark that people for miles can hear
Thin body
Powerful legs
Will kick sand between your legs
This almighty beast
From the east
May be tall
But is the best of them all

It is the greyhound
The best around!

Alyssa Campbell (12)
Lyndon School, Solihull

88

I'M ALWAYS THERE

It's a big world out there,
Never forget me,
How could I ever forget you?
If you look up, I'll be there too,
Looking down on you,
Don't worry, my child,
You might not be able to see me,
But I can see you,
So keep your big, happy smile,
Like you always do,
From your dearest father,
Who loves you.

May Shirley (11)
Lyndon School, Solihull

FUTURE

In the future,
The mighty future,
Will there be flying cars?
Will Donald Trump be behind bars?

In the future,
The mighty future,
Will there be such a thing as snow?
Will Earth be as we know?

In the future,
The mighty future,
Will plastic still be a curse,
Or will there be something worse...?

Benjamin Powell (12)
Lyndon School, Solihull

BODY IMAGE

I stand in front of the mirror,
and the way I look becomes clearer,
my mind dwells on with what I could look like,
and what I could be.

Others are happy, confident,
because they don't look like me.
My self-esteem travels further and further away -
until the eye can't see...

Rhiya Parmar (13)
Lyndon School, Solihull

WATERPARK TROUBLES

Me and my dad
the day was mad
we got lost in the smallest water park in Spain
oh, how it was a pain!
We looked at the map
and my family were on the other side of the park!
We only went to get food
but we found ourselves stuck in a mood.

Millie Samantha Lakin (11)
Lyndon School, Solihull

MY MUM

My mum is the best
Nothing like the rest
I'd be out of my mind
If I didn't think that she was kind
My mum is so nice
She also makes the best rice
Her passion is planting seeds
If you have a mum, she is all you'll ever need.

Heshaam Mahmmud (11)
Lyndon School, Solihull

INNER FEELINGS

It can be lonely
Even when I'm with friends
I still feel alone.

Am I glad or sad?
I don't know what's in my head
Is it good or bad?

When will it be light
Will it become forever dark
Is it only me?

Joshua Bibb (13)
Lyndon School, Solihull

AN ODE TO MY NAN'S DOG

Lily, you're the best dog
You always jump up at me when I come
You are as playful as a little child
Can we not lose you in the snow this year?
Why do you always give me puppy dog eyes?
I love how you are always fluffy.

Amelia Cleverly (11)
Lyndon School, Solihull

BREXIT

Brexit, how bad is Brexit?
Nothing will come out of this for us
All the MPs are bothered about is Brexit
This will end up as a disaster
It's over before the damage is done
Whose idea was it to make Brexit?

Danny Morris (11)
Lyndon School, Solihull

DEPRESSION

He eats away at happiness
He demolishes self-confidence
He brings darkness
He brings fear
He makes you tremble
He makes you cry
He is a threatening monster
He is real
He is depression.

Isha Amaara (12)
Lyndon School, Solihull

AN ODE TO SHINOBI

"Shinobi is annoying,
Shinobi is OP,
Shinobi is ignorant!"
That's what they say to me.
My name is Logan,
I play video games,
My favourite is For Honor,
And Shinobi is my main.

Sam Kell (11) & Logan
Lyndon School, Solihull

AN ODE ABOUT MY DOG

Alfie, you are adorable
greeting me when I get home
rolling on your back
for me to rub your belly.

Owen Gallagher (11)
Lyndon School, Solihull

MY SWEET CONFECTIONERY POEM

In a Galaxy far away,
Second left after the Milky Way,
You'll see a trail of Magic Stars,
That will lead you to the world of chocolate bars.

Deep inside, you will find,
Things that will blow your mind,
With caramel rivers and Freddo frogs,
Jumping over chocolate logs.

With Skittles rainbows and cute Kit Kats,
And scary eyes of chocolate bats,
A candyfloss forest is more than a Turkish delight,
Believe me, the Animal Bars in there are quite a sight.

From gummy worms to gummy bears,
Leave them there if you care,
Have no fear,
Because I am here.

Just follow the path of sherbet dip,
But do not put the sweets to your lip,
For the Lion Bar waits silently,
To attack you violently.

To avoid this terrible creature,
Listen to the words of a Crunchie preacher,
Wispa to this Lion Bar in his large ear,
And away will go all sense of fear.

This leaves you to continue on your path,
When you can have a Snicker and laugh,
There, I will be waiting for you,
With a box of Heroes and Celebrations too.

But this Curly Wurly journey must come to an end,
Go down the road right to the Bassetts bend,
And away you will fly,
And I will wish you goodbye.

Farewell, my friend, as I don't like long goodbyes,
Watch out for your Kinder Surprise!

Tamzin Timperley (12)
St Francis Of Assisi Catholic Technology College, Aldridge

COMIC LAND

Have you ever wished for something more?
A hope, a dream to distract from the bore?
In an Earth-like land and an ordinary town,
The people there, they feel let down,
That the life they once looked at with fascination,
Is now filled with stress and temptation,
Experiencing life first-hand,
Why can't we live in Comic Land?

But one day in one big flash,
These limitations came down with a bash,
Every person found something new,
A superpower unique to you.
With new possibilities at hand,
It then became Comic Land!

They look at the world through the eyes of a child,
They can do whatever and go wild!
With this discovery, new occupations appear,
Being a hero of justice or a villain to be feared...
Action and destruction around every corner of the streets,
Just like the comics that look bound to the sheets.
But is this getting out of hand?
The lives we wished for, Comic Land...

Powers can turn your world on its head,
And in the wrong hands, one might end up dead.
Mischief, havoc and certainly confusion,
These powers might not bring a pretty conclusion.
So next time, think twice about what you wish for,
Of what you desire might be outside the front door.
Think past the comics and what you had planned,
A hope, a dream!
Past Comic Land...

Chloe Birtwistle (12)
St Francis Of Assisi Catholic Technology College, Aldridge

MY BIRTHDAY POEM

The day had finally come
after 364 days of waiting...
I woke up very early
ready for the day!
Did I want it to end?
Oh gosh, no way!
Back to the morning
down the stairs, I did go
I walked into the sitting room
and there I saw a bow.
There was something else, a big thirteen
I had to open the box before my gift could be seen.
All around the house were decorations
it was time for all of the celebrations.
Time to see what's in the box
it might have just been a pair of socks.
I was going to give it a little shake
until I found out it was a birthday cake.
Rainbows, sprinkles, I had it all
I was having a real ball.
Hanging from the ceiling were many balloons
then it was time to start playing some tunes.
Out came the candles
onto the cake, they did go
we sang 'Happy Birthday'
and candles went out with a blow.

To finish celebrations, a party I had
when the day was over, I felt quite sad.
Another year older, a long wait ahead...
"364 days," I said.

Erin McIntyre (12)
St Francis Of Assisi Catholic Technology College, Aldridge

SOMETHING LURKING OUT THERE

If ever you find this secret note,
Then you'd better hope,
They don't see you,
They don't hear you,
But who are they?
I will tell you... but tell no one,
I mean no one!

Are you alone? Okay,
Now that you've opened this secret note,
I'll tell you something very important,
Monsters are lurking everywhere,
You'll know because of their wiry hair,
Their red, bloodshot eyes,
Catch you by surprise,
If they ever find you,
Just beware, for they are everywhere.

Their claws will rip you to a thousand pieces,
As their temper increases,
Before I go,
I must tell you of a time long ago,
When the outbreak of the monsters began,

But fear now,
For they are here now,
Listening and learning the ways of our life,
They only eat with a sharp, metallic knife,
I must now flee,
For they are coming after me!

But heed my word,
It's not that you've not ever heard,
Of a monster!
Beware, little one, beware.

James Wilkinson (11)
St Francis Of Assisi Catholic Technology College, Aldridge

MAGIC LAND

Welcome to my magic land,
Let's start with our wonderful band,
They have some guitars that they put in their cars,
They add their speakers and fill their bottle up with litres,
We have so many wizards,
Special rocks that turn into lizards,
We can hear most people's thoughts,
Because it's warm, people wear shorts,
Someone even grew some claws,
And the animals have paws,
Everyone uses their magical wands,
All of us nearly make magic in a pond,
The food doesn't really taste good enough,
When we are stuffed, we huff and puff,
Our houses are like little mushrooms,
On special nights, we light some fumes,
On Christmas night, we don't get much snow,
And our tradition is to play fairy polo,
On Halloween, it's quite spooky,
We go out and it's really smokey,
This is the end of my magical land,
Make sure to go out and create this magical land in sand,
Magic Land is the perfect place to be,
Well, only if you like magic,
We shall see.

Poppy Fleming (11)
St Francis Of Assisi Catholic Technology College, Aldridge

POET LAND

Here, where the poets sleep,
Right in their beds so, so deep,
Deeply engrossed in their new poem, biography or novel,
While sitting in their tiny hovels,
Hardly any space to move,
Waiting for people to approve.

Let's all remember William Shakespeare,
An amazing poet at heart,
He is known all over the land,
More people know him than grains of sand,
For sure, he was a talented writer,
But let's all remember that he was a poet, not a fighter!

William Shakespeare, with the thous and the thys,
In some of his plays, many people died,
His forte was definitely tragedy,
I wonder if he went to an academy?
For all those great skills he possessed,
I wonder if he looked good in a sparkly dress?

Poetry is a good way to express yourself,
Make sure you don't share your secrets to the Christmas elf!
Go down into your heart and maybe you'll see,
An inner poet lying within thee!

Benita Jaeneke (12)
St Francis Of Assisi Catholic Technology College, Aldridge

MY SUGARY DREAM

My life, my life is so high,
that's why, sometimes, I think of sweet pie.
I feel sugar rushing through my brain,
whilst thinking of some nice Christmas canes.
I feel sugar pouring down my thin body,
whilst my mum screams, "You'd better hurry!"
Sugar makes me feel so crazy,
that's why my dad faints and screams, "Oh, Mary!"
Whilst at school,
my teachers think I'm cool,
because I'm just like a rolling pool.
Pink shoes, pink hair, pink is everywhere!
Well, usually my friends say, "I don't care!"
Well, while the sun shines on a can of cola,
I think my new name is going to be Lola!
Chewy Skittles are everywhere, they make me feel ill,
because they taste my nan's pills!
Don't worry, she still hasn't realised that,
I've dropped them on top of the hill!

Esther Enuoma (11)
St Francis Of Assisi Catholic Technology College, Aldridge

THE LAND OF FORTNITE

Fortnite players and streamers are everywhere,
dying left, right and centre,
like the default over there.
Once you're inside the Battle Bus,
mark a place to land.
Once you have arrived at your destination,
don't just stare and stand.

To win, you must have the ability to survive,
by getting guns, healables and materials,
which will help you to keep alive.
Check on the map to see when the storm is coming,
if you're too far from the circle,
then you'd better start running.

If you take damage from the storm,
heal up and build a base.
If you stand in the middle of the open,
you could possibly get sniped in the face.
When it's down to one v one,
get out your best gun.
Keep shooting until 'Victory Royale' pops up,
which means that you have won!

Hayden Ho (11)
St Francis Of Assisi Catholic Technology College, Aldridge

WAR LAND

War Land - you don't want to go there,
Unless you can face a mighty scare!

Thud! Thud! is all you hear, trudging in the squelchy mud.
"Over the top!" calls a voice, then...
Bang! Bang! Scream! is all you hear,
Even in your dream.

Behind the leader,
Blistered soldiers try to look eager.
Bang! You watched as another one fell,
Now you keep losing them in this treacherous hell!

Then gas bombs surround you like Death's coat,
Wrapping its arms around everyone's throat.
Men begin to fall all over the place,
As your friends die right under your face.

Stepping over body parts,
People are wheeled away in smelly carts.

Soldiers die day after day,
Will war ever end?
Well, that's what you pray...

Lily Sarah Quinn (11)
St Francis Of Assisi Catholic Technology College, Aldridge

SNOW AND ICE

Through a mystical place I go
Bringing curiosity to my mind
I find a small village filling up with snow
Heavy snow lies on each and every branch up above
Disappearing sky, no gleam of sun, just glistening
snowflakes
Delicately dancing through the air
Blanket of white so untouched and crystal-like
So precious, so fragile, so beautiful

Every tree is buried deep in the snow
No flower blooming, nor animals moving
Unusual shapes of icicles surround me
Somewhere has never been so soundless
So precious, so fragile, so beautiful

Every child's dream to see a snowflake fall
And to have the taste of ice touch their tongue
The happiness winter brings
So precious, so fragile, so beautiful...

Sophie Doocey (13)
St Francis Of Assisi Catholic Technology College, Aldridge

HOW I LOVE FOOD

Oh, how I love food,
The delicious burgers,
And the sour sweets,
All I want to buy is that lovely chocolate,
Oh yes, I love food.

Oh, how I love food,
The heart-warming feeling,
Of gathering round the table to eat food,
Until our tummies are full,
Oh yes, I love food.

Oh, how I love food,
I once dreamed of a place,
That was made out of food,
Burgers as houses,
Pizzas as churches,
That is how much I love food.

How much do I love food,
I wake up and eat food,
I go to school and eat food,
I go home and eat food,
Yes, I love food.

How I love food,
Even the simple things like,
Ham sandwiches, fruit and cereal,
I will eat it all because,
I love food!

Charlie Adams (12)
St Francis Of Assisi Catholic Technology College, Aldridge

YoungWriters Est. 1991

FEARS, FEARS!

Fears, fears,
You give me tears,
Spiders, snakes, all over the place.

Spiders crawl,
Snakes hiss,
Poisonous frogs that you can't miss.

As the time passes by,
And the floorboards creak,
It still gives me the creeps.

It's almost Halloween and time to scream,
You will get scared,
So be prepared.

My heart went to my mouth,
As I ran toward the south,
I didn't realise the beast was there,
he had no fur, but just slime...

Then I realised it was a snake!
It made me shake, it made me scream,
I thought to myself, *why am I screaming?*
It's just a slither, slimy snake, no need to fear!

Megan Amstrong (11)
St Francis Of Assisi Catholic Technology College, Aldridge

DRAGON MANIA

In Dragon Mania, the world is at peace,
It has no troubles, nor any geese.
I can escape to this land to fly away,
The world seems so far away.

The dragons here are not crazed,
You will be amazed,
After you ride on a dragon's back,
There are many dragons that are black.

This land has many caves,
We should not have a rave,
The plants are curled,
The houses swirled.

We should care for this dimension,
For we stand to attention,
While these loyal creatures lumber,
They protect us while we slumber,
This ancient dreamland was created by my imagination,
And this is my world.

Harriet Fisher (11)
St Francis Of Assisi Catholic Technology College, Aldridge

LIPSTICK LAND!

Lipstick Land is pretty,
So many colours, not all sticky,
Bright, shiny, glossy and fun,
There's a colour and shade for everyone!

MAC make the matte,
Maybelline make the glitter,
NARS make 3D stars that stand out,
On your pout!

Shades, shades, there are so many shades,
From pink, to purple,
To red, to brown,
There are so many lipsticks to be found!

Superdrug, Boots,
They sell them all,
So get yourself,
To a shopping mall!

I love Lipstick Land,
I hope you do too,
So pucker up with your fave lippy on,
Next time you go to a do!

Annie Hattersley (13)
St Francis Of Assisi Catholic Technology College, Aldridge

HALLOWEEN TOWN

In this town, don't be happy now,
There's a green fluid that will burn your skin,
If the monsters catch you, they will take you to their
pumpkin king.
He'll take you to the fountain where you'll burn,
The monsters will praise you, saying,
"This is Halloween, this is Halloween,
Make a new pumpkin for us, Pumpkin King!"
As you can see, this town is quite horrible,
You should not ever want to come here,
The houses are covered in cobwebs,
Spider as big as a rider,
Creaking floors as you walk into the house,
Now, don't get grabbed by me under the stairs!

Ethan Meers (11)
St Francis Of Assisi Catholic Technology College, Aldridge

SNOW AND ICE LAND

I went to bed early last night,
And when I woke, all I saw was white.
I stood on the ground,
It made a big crunching sound.

I had gloves on my hands,
Whilst the ice melted on the lands.
The road ahead was extremely steep,
And the snow was oh so deep.

I've had the most wonderful day,
Because all I had was the snow and ice to play.
As it started to sleet,
I knew I should go to sleep.

It kept building up on freezing ground,
Hiding all and muffling sound.
But, in time, the snow plough cleared the road,
Sadly, bits of grass started to show.

Jessica Munslow (12)
St Francis Of Assisi Catholic Technology College, Aldridge

ENCHANTED WOOD

Through the gate to the enchanted wood,
Elves, fairies in the flower flood.
Stumbling through, watch out for the bear,
Instead, being surprised by the magic sparkling in the air.
Rainbows shining through the trees,
Suddenly, you hear a magical song,
Thinking how you could be here all day long.
Looking at the flowers growing so proud,
Suddenly, you see a crowd,
A crowd of mice and rabbits and deer,
All listening with their ears.
There, there, there, over there,
Under that tree,
Fairies and elves, butterflies and ladybirds,
All dancing with glee!

Freya Coyne (11)
St Francis Of Assisi Catholic Technology College, Aldridge

FLOWER LAND

In my land, we love to play,
We can play all day!
I like to go to sniff the flowers,
It is like they have magic powers.
The flowers like to sleep under the trees,
And then feed on leaves.
In the day, there is sun,
We can have so much fun!
In this land, people smile!
Come to my world and stay for a while.
In my land, money grows on trees,
And you don't get stung by bees!
In this magical land, you don't have to work,
But you are free to twerk.
In this flower mansion, you can have any food,
And you will stay in a happy mood.

Charlotte Freeth (11)
St Francis Of Assisi Catholic Technology College, Aldridge

MARIO KART WORLD

In Mario Kart World,
Everybody races,
Against new faces,
You collect a lot of items,
While learning how to find them.

But, before you start,
You'll have to pick your kart,
After that, I like to pick Luigi,
Because he is very greedy,
With his red shells,
He says farewell,
To the losers of the race.

So it doesn't matter if you are good or bad,
It doesn't matter if you are a girl or a lad,
But it does matter that you like to play Mario Kart,
And if you want to be the winner, you've got to play it
smart!

Harry J Bradbury (11)
St Francis Of Assisi Catholic Technology College, Aldridge

SUGAR LAND

When you are feeling lonely and depressed
you can come down to Sugar Land instead
gazing into the sky, I can see pink clouds
watch out for the tickle sweets, they make you LOL!

You can come here to forget about your sorrows
and maybe stay here till tomorrow
Sugar Land has everything
and maybe some unexpected treats.

It has chocolate ice cream and even chocolate mousse
which delight would you choose?
If you hurry, you might get a treat
not oat, porridge or wheat.

Visit the sugar delight store
You won't be ignored!

Shantel Odera Dike (11)
St Francis Of Assisi Catholic Technology College, Aldridge

FRIENDSHIP FOREST

In Friendship Forest, all are greeted,
The comfiest chair is where you are seated,
Houses are filled with glitz and bling,
Colours that will make your heart sing.

No alarms are needed in here,
You'll be so happy you won't shed a tear,
Whenever you need it, your hand will be held,
With smells so sweet, no one's repelled.

Campfires and marshmallows every night,
There is never a hug out of sight,
I want to be there, I'll be honest,
This is what it's like in Friendship Forest.

Millie Anne Kilgallen (13)
St Francis Of Assisi Catholic Technology College, Aldridge

THE UNDERWATER LAND

A whole new world lies under the sea,
Shoals of fish swim majestically across the sea.
Amongst the brightly coloured fish is where I want to be,
Just somewhere I can be free.
Overlooking the stars, the crystal-clear water twinkles like pearls,
Calm and peaceful, the waves silently swirl.
Big fish, small fish, yellow fish, blue fish and purple fish are all I can see,
Multi-coloured coral and large creatures are all that surround me.
How beautiful is this place, a secret hideaway,
A place I can go to ponder every day.

Elizah-Hannah Haroon (11)
St Francis Of Assisi Catholic Technology College, Aldridge

FOOD FEST

Food Fest is the place to be...

When you go into the Fast Food Quarter
Make sure you place the biggest order
Get your fries in any size
You can order a drink and it'll be there in a blink

The Healthy Hut is the place to be
Nutritional food is definitely key
Healthy options make you your best
Fruit and veg, forget the rest

Never forget the Dessert Den
After your main, pop in then
Sugar and sweetness in every treat
Such a cool place to sit down and eat!

Eireann Mae Brannigan (11)
St Francis Of Assisi Catholic Technology College, Aldridge

FAIRY TALE FOREST

Fairy Tale Forest is full of magic and dreams,
In Fairy Tale Forest, nothing is what it seems,
Pixies and fairies dance around,
Gumdrops and lollipops cover the ground.

Each day, a new chapter,
An atmosphere full of happiness and laughter,
Little people living in a tree,
Singing and shouting with glee.

The sound of the twinkling bells,
Friendly trolls casting spells,
All the magical characters you can think of,
The ones we all adore and love.

Megan Barton (13)
St Francis Of Assisi Catholic Technology College, Aldridge

GAMING LAND

G aming is really fun, I can do it all day
A good thing we live here too
M y mum is the best
I go outside to play with my friends
N eil goes to the portal and jumps in, I
G o into the best portal and get to a good land

L oving every second, I play till I'm dead
A nd I get home, eat my dinner and go to sleep
N ight is here and I'm now dead, this
D ay has been fun, tomorrow is another.

Aleksander Graczkowski (11)
St Francis Ot Assisi Catholic Technology College, Aldridge

FORTNITE

Fortnite, we are gonna play it all night!
We drop from the bus into a wonderful land,
For a Victory Royale, it has to be planned.
1000 IQ, you need it to win,
If you don't have that, you're committing a sin.
So do it, go out there, fight for your life,
You'll regret it if you don't,
Then you'll realise your strife,
And yes, the island is extremely big,
But always remember, only ninety-nine problems of which to
get rid.

Matthew John Logan (11)
St Francis Of Assisi Catholic Technology College, Aldridge

THE OCEAN

The ocean is a very vast place,
At the top, small fish sway their fins,
At the bottom, huge monsters lurk.

This place is our home,
A huge aquarium shaped like a dome,
Every day, see people lay,
Around our home, staring in awe.

Great fish, towering kelp,
Miniature fish, some inflate, some sink,
Some make shells to sleep.

Many predators,
Much prey,
Some extinct,
Some alive,
Some... behind you!

Joel Mulligan (11)
St Francis Of Assisi Catholic Technology College, Aldridge

CANDY SNOW CITY

In Candy Snow City,
Everything's pretty,
It's all delicious here,
Christmas is all the time here.

Snow is all around us,
Which you can eat,
It's amazing all year round,
Houses are made out of ice cream and candy,
There is no school here at all.

The trees are covered with snow,
All the children are cheerful here,
Come and visit this place,
Where you can have fun and stuff your face.

Megan Banks (12)
St Francis Of Assisi Catholic Technology College, Aldridge

LEARNING LAND

The Learning Land is strict
Especially if you get picked.
The floor is a book
Why don't you take a look
At the ink river down the crease in the book?

The trees are made of pencil
The branches made of lead
The little houses made of rubber
Quite cosy when going to bed.

The words will come to life
Vocabulary running round, crazy
The morning sun is hazy
As I am in bed, feeling lazy.

Jarlaith Hitchings (11)
St Francis Of Assisi Catholic Technology College, Aldridge

FROST LAND

In Frost Land, everything is cold
But you'll think it's gold
It's all icy and blue
It's magic for you!

Everyone's fantastic
You could even say they are enthusiastic
Merry and bright
It's really annoying, it will give you a fright!

Sent from Heaven, snowflakes
Keep a handful as a keepsake
Wet pockets you will get
But fantastic memories you will never forget!

Violet-May Green (12)
St Francis Of Assisi Catholic Technology College, Aldridge

FIRE LAND

As a fire burns in your soul,
You will never get cold.
The burning light moves from place to place,
And you will always have space.
You will never get burned,
As you move around and turn.

Everything is made of fire,
And nobody will ever call you a liar.
Burning flames light up your mood,
And you will never be rude.

Fire, fire, fire is all you see,
But you will never see me...

Marypeace Osazuwa (11)
St Francis Of Assisi Catholic Technology College, Aldridge

FOOD WORLD

In Food World, people are weird
and everywhere is chocolate-smeared
hanging from trees are burger buns
with people starting to fill their tums
take your hotdog out for a walk and a dip
and if you get an ice cream, let him have a lick
in my Food World, everything has good taste
and I guarantee none of it goes to waste.

If we have whet your appetite
why not come and visit us tonight?

Katie Martindale (12)
St Francis Of Assisi Catholic Technology College, Aldridge

LAND OF CAKE

In the Land of Cake,
There's nothing you can't bake,
Everything is sweet,
There is always a treat.

The houses are soft and spongy,
Have a bite if you are hungry,
There are rivers filled with cream,
Licking it feels like a dream.

The air smells like heaven,
When the cake is out of the oven,
Endless cake, lots of sugar,
Eat them all and you'll feel hyper!

Alisha Karunanayake (12)
St Francis Of Assisi Catholic Technology College, Aldridge

CANDY LAND POEM

C andy Land is a great place to live
H ouses made from gingerbread
O nly the best candyfloss in the world
C an make you feel so in the zone!
O h, in this land, anyone can live
L and of candy is never a bad thing
A nd marshmallow trees
T hat blow in the breeze
E veryone wants to come back once they have visited
before!

Ruby Wood (12)
St Francis Of Assisi Catholic Technology College, Aldridge

HALLOWEEN SCARE

This Halloween's scary,
the night is dark,
though the children don't bite,
they look like witches,
they live in ditches,
spooky, small creature,
knocks on the door,
but all they hear are people that roar,
"Trick or treat!" they say,
I smell their sweets,
but don't make a tweet.

Serena Nunda (12)
St Francis Of Assisi Catholic Technology College, Aldridge

IN CANDY LAND

In Candy Land,
Nightmares are banned,
Candy is everywhere,
It might be in your hair!
The clouds are pink,
It may make you think,
Are they candyfloss?
Well, the answer is yes!
The gummy snakes make a mess.

It is totally random,
In Candy Land!

Lilly Stone (11)
St Francis Of Assisi Catholic Technology College, Aldridge

LIFE'S JOURNEY

Take all the present joy there is
in sunshine and in showers.
Tomorrow's in the hands of God
today alone is ours.

And let the future rest with him
with every anxious care.
You'll find that as you journey on
he's with you everywhere.

Corben Oakley (12)
St Francis Of Assisi Catholic Technology College, Aldridge

LAND OF THE FIREWORKS

Every day is bonfire night for me...
I hear big bangs every night and children having fun.
I see the fireworks zoom up and then explode.
I smell the burning fire.
I taste the smoke of the burning flames.
I touch the misty fog.
I love Bonfire Night!

Oliver Ogbeide (11)
St Francis Of Assisi Catholic Technology College, Aldridge